THE BASICS OF NINJA SCALPING

HOW TO TRADE USD/JPY AND GROW YOUR ACCOUNT BY 10% MONTHLY

J.P. BAUTISTA

For Carlo, Cara, and Miguel

ISBN: 9781724117458
Independently published

CONTENTS

INTRODUCTION

Trading forex is exhilarating. And it attracts individuals who are thrill seekers. This being the case, entering transactions just to get a rush will most likely cause a trader to lose money. A quote from Ed Seykota goes, *"There are old traders and there are bold traders, but there are very few old, bold traders."* I agree wholeheartedly.

People who follow a proven trading method are the ones who profit and live off their earnings in the long run. Though there are those who have amassed great wealth from a single lucky trade, market participants who treat trading as gambling are the ones who blow their accounts sooner or later. Every trader should treat forex trading as a business. Protect capital, manage risk, and have realistic profit targets. Do these and you'll see steady, measurable, and *sustainable* growth.

With this strategy, our goal is to enter the market at the right time, with the right conditions in place, and to exit as soon as we've achieved our intraday goal. We don't intend to pick tops and bottoms, ride the trend, maximize profits, and so forth. If that's what you're looking for, you'll be better off putting this book down and looking for one better suited for your personal goals.

Before we proceed, I must emphasize:

- A trading system is indispensable for long-term success.
- It must work; no use following a strategy that's flawed.
- When you find an effective technique, adhere to it, no matter what your emotions tell you.

If in day-to-day trading, you cannot tick off all three items on this list, you're bound to lose everything to the markets. The technique is easy enough to learn in one sitting, but what will be most important is having the resolve to stick to your guns when it matters.

THE NINJA SCALPING METHOD

In this book, I will provide specific steps on how to trade the US Dollar against the Japanese Yen. Foreign currency traders often refer to them as the USD/JPY pair. **Ninja Scalping is a proven, profitable trading system, from which you can earn an average of 10% profit per month.** You can withdraw all profits as extra income or roll it over to the next month to build a substantial nest egg. Alternatively, you can withdraw a portion of the monthly profits and realize them, then roll over the rest so that your equity continually grows.

This method is loosely based on the techniques discussed by Mark Fisher in The Logical Trader: A Method to the Madness. It was the first trading book I ever picked up and remains the most useful book I have ever read on the topic. Since Fisher's method focuses more on commodities trading, I made adjustments to suit those who want to trade the USD/JPY pair. This is a trading system designed to get you in and out of the market as quickly but as cautiously possible, with profit in your pocket and a smile on your face when you go to bed.

FOR THE NEWBIE

Capital

Question: How much do you need to invest?

Answer: Invest an amount you can afford to lose without breaking down emotionally. It must be an amount that does not jeopardize your present and future financial security. What amount comes to your mind when the phrase "chump change" is floated? That is the exact amount you need to invest in your first forex venture. Remember, you may slip up along the way, but you'll want to avoid making costly mistakes. You should be able to chalk up early mishaps as battle losses but they must not cost you the war. It is easier to add capital later than to struggle to recoup losses you could have prevented by not being over-aggressive.

Learn the Basics

There is a profusion of materials readily available on the basics of forex trading. I am a strong believer in efficiency and showing you where to look for the information would be more helpful than for me to write a whole section on the basics.

You can go to https://www.babypips.com/learn/forex/preschool. Getting through the preschool and kindergarten portions of their comprehensive courses would be enough for our purposes. If you want to immerse yourself in learning everything you can, kudos to you! Do it. (It's totally free).

Often, brokers have their own training material on their websites which aim to orient beginners. That's also a good way to go.

Opening a demo account will help you adapt to your trading platform safely. Even if you make a mistake while practicing how to make trades, it won't be with real money. You can even try Ninja Scalping on your demo account to prove that it works before you try it with your own money.

Once you've learned the lingo, how to interpret a candlestick chart, how to navigate your trading platform, and how to set up and close trades, you can move on to the next step.

If you have no or little prior knowledge about forex trading, I strongly advise you to take the steps above (especially the first one) before you go on any further. If you don't have at least a working knowledge of the basics, the latter part of this book won't make much sense to you.

Open an Account

There are hundreds of brokers out there. Nowadays, it's so easy to open an account. You can trade for as low as $50. Majority of brokers even give bonuses just for depositing money and/or entering a trade.

To open an account, you'll need a valid passport or any other government-issued ID, proof of billing, and a bank account, credit card, or electronic wallet (i.e., Skrill) to deposit/withdraw funds. Other requirements may be necessary on a per country basis, but they should be easy to comply with. Once you've set up an account, and your broker has validated it, you're good to go.

Pro Tip: You can go to www.investing.com/brokers/forex-brokers. They have a list of legitimate brokers, and a description of the minimum deposit required, usual spread, and other details in the broker profile. This will help you make an informed decision about which broker to use.

When you open an account, your broker may ask you the amount of leverage you want. A leverage of 1:50 or 1:100 would be suitable for our purposes.

If you're starting with a capital of less than $5000, choose Micro Lot when you're asked to choose among Standard, Mini or Micro.

THE MEAT OF THE MATTER

There is nothing left to discretion using the Ninja Scalping method. Every step is clearly defined. If you're in this to make money, follow the path and it won't let you down. However, if you're in this for the thrill of winning when you're right about a hunch, I guarantee that you'll ignore the rules once you see that first big spike or dip in the price. If that's how it plays out, I hope Lady Luck doesn't display her renowned fickleness to you too soon. If you do blow your account, here's what to do:

-   Take time off from trading (a week at least).
-   Let your emotions settle.
-   Gather capital you can afford to lose.
-   Read this very short book again.
-   Restart trading.

By this time, I hope you would have learned that sticking to a trading system is necessary for your survival in the markets. Playing your hunches will take you out of the game faster than you can say WTF.

Plot the Opening Range

Find the 30-minute candle that corresponds to **9:00 am to 9:30 am Tokyo time**. Mark the highest and lowest prices with a pair of horizontal lines. This is your opening range.

Figure 1 - Opening range upper and lower lines

Plot the Breakout Lines

Plot out another horizontal line 80 points above the higher range and another one 80 points below the lower range. We will call these lines your upper and lower breakout lines, respectively. For example, the extremes of prices between 9:00 to 9:30 are 112.831 and 112.722. The upper breakout line would be plotted at 112.911 and the lower breakout line would be plotted at 112.642.

Note: I use the term "point" in this book to mean 1 thousandth or 0.001. So, 80 points would be equal to 0.080.

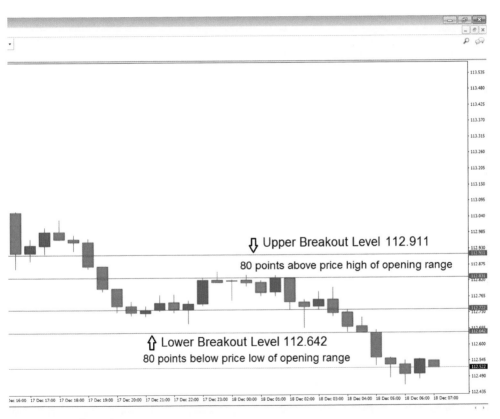

Figure 2 - Breakout Lines

Wait for the Signal

Wait for the price to break out either above or below the opening range. It should stay at least 15 minutes above or below your breakout line. A 15-minute candle close above or below the breakout line while waiting for signal confirmation is a good sign. A 30-minute or hourly candle close beyond the breakout line during your waiting period is even better. Sometimes, the price moves to the breakout line then pulls back and then touches it again. That is okay, too. What is most important to remember is that the total time in between the two touches must be at least 15 minutes for it to count. Once this criterion is satisfied, you have the go signal to enter a trade.

Figure 3 - Confirmed Signal

Pro Tip: Most trading platforms have a feature that allows you to set up an audible alarm when the price reaches a certain level. Learn how to do this and it can save you hours of staring at the screen, waiting for the price to break out. Investing.com has a phone app you can install on your mobile. You can set up alerts to go straight to your phone.

Figure 4 - Alerts

Entry Points

For a buy trade, the entry point is 50 points below your upper breakout line. Using our previous example with the upper breakout line at 112.911, the entry point would be at 112.861. For a sell trade, it is 50 points above the lower breakout line. With the lower breakout line being 112.642, the entry point for a sell trade would be 112.692.

Note: Sometimes the breakout is so strong that the price is not able to retrace 50 points from the breakout line. On a day like this, it is not wrong to place a trade right at the breakout level as long as you have a confirmed signal. It results in taking a higher risk and a lower profit, so enter at this level only on trending days where the candles are big and solid, moving in the direction of your trade. Adjust your lot size so that the risk taken is never greater than 2% of capital (more on how to adjust position size in a later chapter).

Figure 5 - Entry Points

Stop Losses

For a buy trade, the stop loss would be 10 points below lower breakout line or 112.632. For a sell trade, it would be 10 points above the upper breakout line or 112.921.

Pro Tip: NEVER flip-flop on stop loss levels. If you're wrong, you're wrong. Take the loss. Do not hold on to losing positions. There will always be another opportunity.

Figure 6 - Stop Losses

Take Profit Levels

For a buy trade, the take profit level would be 150 points above the upper breakout line at 113.061. For a sell trade, it would be 150 points below the lower breakout line at 112.492.

On days when you decide that entering at the breakout point is worth it, if there is a fundamental indication (relevant news) that supports a sustained move, you can adjust your take profit level 50 points beyond the usual to compensate for the adjusted entry point.

At the time of writing, volatility in the forex market is way down. The 20-day average daily range is only around 500 points for USD/JPY. Two years ago, it was averaging 800 to 1000 points a day. When volatility comes back to those levels, increasing your target points to 200, even to 250, should be a good way to increase profitability. But at the current state of volatility, 150 points is a safe target.

I set a profit target because I like to "set and forget." I don't like being trapped in front of the screen, watching the markets all day, looking for signs that the trend is about to reverse. I end up making stupid, emotion-based decisions. Also, a defined target allows me to enjoy the benefits of working from home (or the beach), which was what attracted me to trading in the first place. One can argue that profits are not maximized, but that's the price I'm willing to pay for freedom. As mentioned earlier, we do not aim to ride trends. The goal is to take our daily piece of the pie and run with it.

Figure 7 - Take Profit Levels

Enter the Trade

One way is to wait for the price to reach your entry point and enter a buy or sell trade. Make sure to always enter your stop loss and take profit levels. Use this method if the price moves to your desired entry level soon after a go signal is generated.

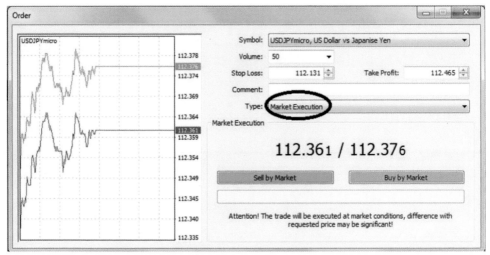

Figure 8 – Enter a Market Execution Trade

If it's taking its own sweet time, you can enter a limit order. A buy or sell limit order is an order to purchase a security at a particular price, allowing you to specify a price you will transact. Again, enter your stop loss and take profit levels along with the entry price. All trading platforms have this feature and it should not be difficult to find out how to do it. You can always ask your broker's support team for help in navigating your platform.

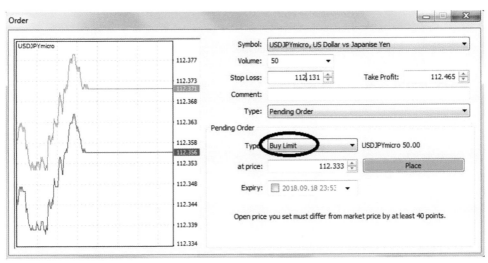

Figure 9 - Enter Limit Order

Let the System Work

Once you've entered the order, move away from your screen. Staring at it will make you vulnerable to temptation and emotional responses. Trust in the system. Do not give in!

When to Cancel the Limit Order

If you entered a trade via market execution (a.k.a. a buy or a sell order in real-time), well and good. You can just go ahead with your day and trust for the system to do its job.

If you entered a limit order, eight to ten hours after you've set it, open your platform again. If the trade has been triggered, just let the trade run its course.

If it still hasn't been triggered, go to the 1-hour time frame chart and insert the parabolic SAR (PSAR) indicator. Several dots will appear across your chart. If you have a buy order, check that your entry price is still above the most current dot. If it is already below the dot, cancel the order and consider it a no-trade day. If you have a sell order, your entry price should still be below the PSAR dot on the 1-hour time frame chart. Cancel the order if the entry price is already above the dot.

Figure 10 - PSAR

System Failure and How to Minimize Losses

Ninja Scalping primarily works in a trending market and routinely fails in a ranging market. The average directional index (ADX) is a trend strength indicator. Regardless of trend direction, it goes up when there is a strong trend and goes down as trend strength decreases. A value above 25 would show good trend strength. The 4-hour timeframe ADX works as the best indicator of trend strength in relation to the Ninja Scalping System.

Check the 4-hour chart ADX value each day. You can find it on your trading platform among the indicators routinely provided. If it is below 25, then you should pause and weigh your options. I do not recommend using the system in the traditional manner on low-ADX days. You can opt to stay out of the market altogether. That is the safest way to go.

On ranging days when the ADX is below 25, I have tried using the breakout lines to sell high and buy low. I must say the experiment has gone fairly well. With a low ADX, there is a weak trend in place but it's still there. The trend is bullish when the 4-hour Relative Strength Index (RSI) is above 50. The trend is bearish when the 4-hour RSI is below 50. I would still want to trade in the trend's direction, however weak it may be.

If I'm looking primarily to sell, I wait for the price to reach the upper breakout level. If the current upward move is showing signs of weakness, I sell from there. The profit target is the lower breakout level. Stop loss is 150 points above the upper breakout level. If I'm looking to buy, then I do the exact opposite. This is a more apt game plan for range-bound trading. This approach has not only minimized loss days, it has caused me to profit from what would have been unprofitable days.

As a precautionary measure, before I take a trade, I look at the longer-term supports and resistances.

Consider this scenario. The ADX is high. Price action has been trending. The breakout level is reached quickly and confidently. But the trade ends up a loser. What could possibly be the cause?

Check the higher timeframe supports and resistances. Price action might be on the verge of hitting a brick wall, and it pays to know if one is just up ahead.

I look at the 200 simple and exponential moving averages on the 4H, Daily, Weekly and Monthly timeframes. Insert these as indicators on your chart. At the very least, price action meeting these lines would cause a short-term bounce. At worst, it can lead to a reversal.

What you can do in cases like these is wait it out. Allow the price action to actually bump into the line, wait for the retracement, and then go in at a better price. If you're hoping it's just a bounce, then entering at a better price would mitigate your risk.

Once the price action hits the moving average and retraces, look at the candle configuration for signs of an actual reversal. Do this on the hourly timeframe. The lower timeframes often give a nonprofitable reversal signal. Remember, a candle must close before you "read" it. A quick spike and reversal that results in a long tail, twin towers, or pincers followed by further price movement against the trend could indicate a reversal.

Further price movement against the trend should be given emphasis. A hammer, pincer or twin tower, however pretty it looks, is irrelevant if price action does not follow through. I wait for price to move 20 more points (or 2 *pips*) before I enter the trade. If these happen though, it's time to switch sides.

Holidays and News Releases

Do not trade on holidays. Always check the economic calendar (https://www.investing.com/economic-calendar/) first thing in the morning. Due to the thin volume on holidays, prices are easily manipulated and you may be caught off guard with huge price swings that reverse quickly and leave you high and dry. Count holidays as no-trade days.

Watch out as well for major news releases, which can increase volatility for a short period. It is best not to enter a trade until after the price action has settled after the news release. Always check the economic calendar for high-impact news especially regarding the US Dollar and Japanese Yen.

Spread

Keep the spread in mind when setting your buy or sell limit. The spread is the difference between the buy price and the sell price. It represents the brokerage service costs. This is how your broker charges you for each trade and makes money. Some brokers charge you the spread upon entering a trade while some charge you upon entering and exiting the trade. Some don't at all but charge a fixed commission. The amount of spread also differs from broker to broker. This is something you have to consider when setting your buy or sell order limits.

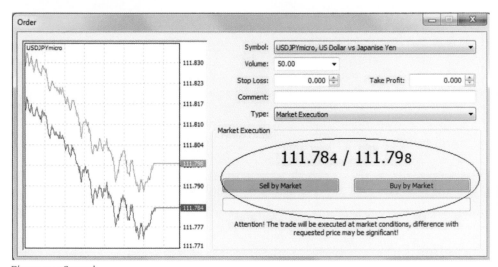

Figure 11 - Spread

For example, a broker charges upon buying. The price breaks upwards and the breakout line is 112.365. Here, you would want to buy 50 points below the breakout line. Your entry point would be 112.315. However, you note that there is an 18-point spread. This means that your buy limit should be entered as 112.333.

Conversely, if the price breaks downward and the breakout line is 112.141, you would want to enter a sell limit at 112.141. You do not adjust for spread because the broker only charges on every buy trade. What you need to do is adjust your take profit level. Since taking profit would technically be a buy trade, that is when the broker will charge the spread. Using our take profit guidelines, it should be at 112.041. Considering the spread, it should be entered on your platform as 112.059.

If you're doing a market execution order, you need not take the spread in consideration upon entering but you need to consider it if the broker will charge you the spread upon exiting.

I know this can be quite confusing on the written page, but once you do a few practice trades on your demo account, you'll understand how to factor in the spread quickly.

Risk

Once you have deposited into your trading account, compute how much 2% of your capital is. That is the maximum acceptable risk for the day. For a thousand-dollar capital, the maximum acceptable risk for the day is $20.

You might ask why it's that low. Forex is inherently risky and anything can happen. Losing several trades in a row is not improbable at all. Keeping the risk at a low rate allows you to live to fight another day.

Keeping the risked capital at a minimum also lessens the emotional investment in a trade. You'll find this to be a key factor in long-term success. This keeps you from being strongly affected by the intraday market swings. Your chances of letting the trade play out to the end, either to a win or a loss, are greater. This, in turn, allows the system to work better overall. Try to liken yourself to a train that chugs slowly but steadily up a hill instead of a race car which pulls to the front of the pack in the beginning but ends up crashing and burning.

Position Sizing

The correct position size will ensure that you achieve the targeted profit for the day and lose only what you can if things go south. There are multiple ways to compute position size, but I've found that the fastest way to do it is just by trial and error. Let me explain:
Use a forex profit/loss calculator like this one: www.oanda.com/forex-trading/analysis/profit-calculator/

- Enter your account currency (what currency you used when you deposited into your trading account). We will assume your account is in USD.
- Choose USD/JPY as the currency pair.
- Leave the Current Price field alone.
- Enter your Entry Point in the Trade Price Field. As an example, let's say 112.315 is our entry level for a buy trade. Adjusting for an 18-point spread, your entry price will actually be 112.333.
- Choose Buy/Long as your Action, assuming that the price broke out upwards.
- Enter a random number in Number of Units. Let's try 5000 for fun.
- Enter your Stop loss as the Closing Price (e.g., 112.131). – Click on Calculate and it will show you that if the trade turns out to be a loss, you'll lose $9.01.

Forex Trading Profit/Loss Calculator

Calculate a trade's profit or loss. Compare the results for different opening and closing rates (either historic or hypothetical).

Profit Calculator

Account Currency	USD ▾
Currency Pair	USD/JPY ▾
Current Price (JPY/USD)	0.0089
Trade Price (USD/JPY)	112.333
Action	Buy/Long ▾
Number of Units	5000
Closing Price	112.131
	Calculate
Profit (USD)	-9.01

Figure 12.1 – Calculator at 5000 units

You will want to use up the maximum allowable daily risk, which is $20 per our example. Play around with the number of units until you come up with a projected loss of $20.

It turns out you must buy 11,100 units so that your trade is limited to a $20 loss. If you have a Micro Lot account, divide 11,100 by 1000 and you'll get 11.100. Round that off to 2 decimal points and you'll get 11.10. That is your correct position size.

If you have a Standard Lot account, you must divide by 100,000. So, your lot size should be 0.11. If you have a Mini Lot account, you must divide by 10,000 and lot size would be 1.1.

Forex Trading Profit/Loss Calculator

Calculate a trade's profit or loss. Compare the results for different opening and closing rates (either historic or hypothetical).

Profit Calculator

Account Currency	USD ▾
Currency Pair	USD/JPY ▾
Current Price (JPY/USD)	0.0089
Trade Price (USD/JPY)	112.333
Action	Buy/Long ▾
Number of Units	11100
Closing Price	112.131
Calculate	
Profit (USD)	-20

Figure 12.2 – Calculator at 11,100 units

Win/Lose Rate

We've talked about risk because the reality is, there is no perfect system. You've got to be ready to take some losses. That is why risk management is key. Taking the cost of trading (spread) into consideration, the risk/reward ratio for this system is roughly 1.2 to 1. Notice that the risk is higher than the reward. This goes against the often repeated trading tenet that the foreseen risk must always be less than the foreseen reward. However, the exceptional win/loss ratio of the system offsets this. For every 20 trading days, there would usually be 11 win days, 4 loss days, and 5 no-trade days. Take note that this is on average, just to give you an idea. There will be months that will be better and months that will be worse than the mean. But even on a cruddy trading cycle with an uptick in loss days, the win/loss rate more than makes up for the shortfall in the risk/reward ratio.

Note: If you've ever studied other mechanical trading systems, you'll find that they often present the risk/reward equation in an idealized way. No cost of trading is factored in and you're left wondering why the technique does not work out as expected in real life. Here, I've put in a whopping 18-point spread in the calculations so you don't get a prettified picture.

AUTHOR'S NOTE

The Ninja Scalping Method has been truly successful in creating an additional income stream for me and my family. Thus, I want to share it with you. I can speak from personal experience that the hardest part is sticking to the plan. When you're down three straight days and likely to end up in the red for the week, it suddenly becomes difficult to remember the rules, much less follow them. Keep in mind that this method will not work if you do not follow the system. Following the method for a couple of days that end up in losses and then giving up on it just when things take a turn is a surefire formula for disaster. Taking profits too early will result in not having enough profit in your pocket to offset the times when a loss is in the cards. Moving stop losses further away can make you risk more than you should. Shifting them nearer to the target can make you vulnerable to sudden dips or spikes that often prove to be scare tactics or "stop loss hunts" by the bigger players. Keeping your cool will prove to be the best thing you can do for your trading account. Let the trades play out their course and trust that the odds are in your favor in the long run.

I thank you for purchasing this book. I sincerely believe it will increase your income and guide you on your journey to financial freedom. I wish you nothing but prosperity and financial security. Happy (but cautious) trading and may you have a long and fulfilling trading career!

DISCLAIMER

Trading foreign exchange carries a high level of risk and may not be suitable for all investors. Past performance is not indicative of future results. The high degree of leverage can work for or against you. Before deciding to invest, carefully consider your investment objectives, level of experience, and risk appetite. The possibility exists that you could sustain a loss of some or all of your initial investment, and therefore, you should not invest funds you cannot afford to lose. Seek advice from an independent financial advisor if you have questions or doubts.

Printed in Great Britain
by Amazon

28079271R00018